Elegant Handcrafted Wreaths

Make Faux Flowers Come Alive
with Breathtaking, Natural Designs

Elegant Handcrafted Wreaths

Stephanie Petrak

Founder of Lorraine's Cottage

Copyright © 2021 Stephanie Petrak

First published in 2021 by

Page Street Publishing Co.

27 Congress Street, Suite 105

Salem, MA 01970

www.pagestreetpublishing.com

Distributed by Macmillan, sales in Canada by The Canadian Manda Group.

25   24   23   22   21   1   2   3   4   5

ISBN-13: 978-1-64567-420-7

ISBN-10: 1-64567-420-7

Library of Congress Control Number: 2021931041

Cover and book design by Meg Baskis for Page Street Publishing Co.

Photography by Sharon Hughes

Printed and bound in China

Page Street Publishing protects our planet by donating to nonprofits like The Trustees, which focuses on local land conservation.

dedication

To my mom, for showing me the joy of a creative life.

Contents

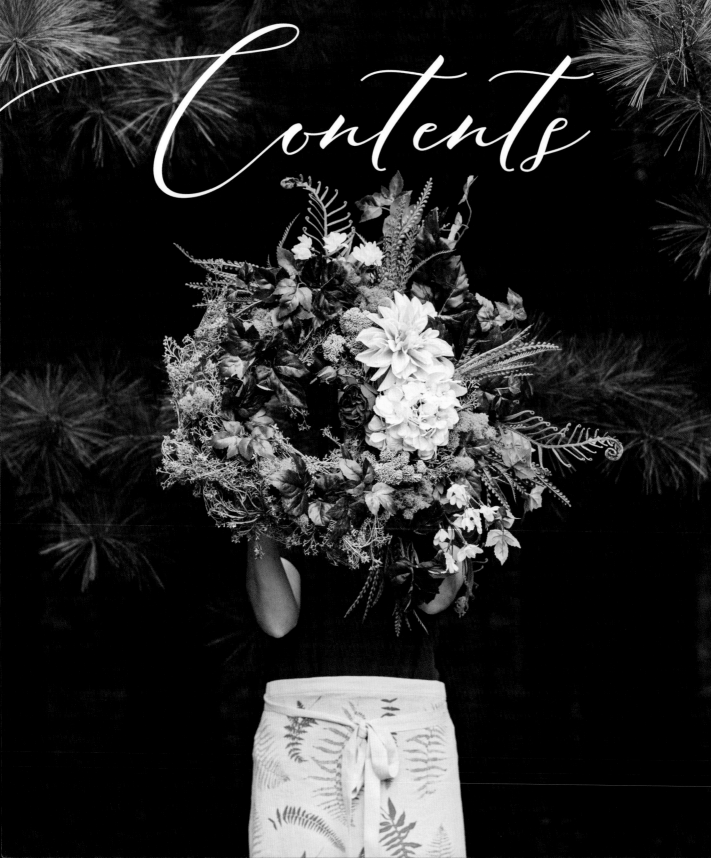

Introduction   9

one

Getting Ready to Create a Wreath   13

The Right Wreath Base   14

Selecting the Best Faux Florals   16

Tools Needed   17

Hanging Your Completed Design   17

two

Wreath Design Foundational Techniques   19

Trimming Materials   21

Design Techniques   22

three

From the Garden   29

The Wedgemere   31
a whimsical take on a classic herb wreath

The Piper   35
striking anemones with soft dusty miller

The Adelaide   41
shabby chic pink florals

The Eccleston   47
extra-large floral statement wreath for large spaces

The Florio   53
ombré pink color story florals

The Avondale   61
a bumper crop of dahlia blooms

The Aria   67
neutral fall florals

The Blomfield   73
sunflowers highlighted by purple greenery

four

From the Woods   79

The Kinley   81
a mixture of ferns focused on shape and movement

The Penley   85
soft, mossy greenery with purple florals

The Cecily   91
free-flowing spring blooming branches and buds

The Sulina   95
leafy fall foliage

The Hollycroft   99
classic winter pine and berries

The Biscay   103
Nordic-inspired evergreen branches

five

From the Field   107

The Ashby   109
a lovely mixture of lush greenery

The Hillside   115
summer wildflowers

The Cottesworth   121
fall berries and pods

The Havenridge   127
everything twiggy, dried and dead for Halloween

The Gloucester   133
Colonial Williamsburg–inspired apple branches among magnolia leaves and berries

The Bramley   137
abundant pumpkins and squash

Acknowledgments   143

About the Author   145

Index   147

Introduction

Have you secretly thought to yourself that in another life, you'd be a florist? That the idea of playing with flowers all day sounds magical? In today's hustle society, the pull to slow down and just create beautiful things is even stronger. Can you feel it?

You don't want to create just any old flower design, though. You want to create with flowers in the artful, free-flowing way seen in popular florists' work today. But where do you start?

What if I told you that you can have a piece of that floral magic in your life now without the time, expense and risk of changing your path, going to floral school and landing a new job as a florist?

Let me introduce you to my whimsical, nature-inspired take on faux floral wreath design for the home creative—completely accessible to any individual, whether just starting out or a seasoned crafter. You just need to love flowers.

I thought I was destined for law school and would work in government. I even completed my undergraduate degree with that intent. When I actually worked in the field of law, my soul was zapped. I felt that pull of creativity and the freedom it brings. I left that job and what I always thought would be my path to pursue working with my hands. Making greeting cards is what I knew, so that was the beginning of my business. But being the creative person I am, I experimented with faux flowers just for fun. I ended up creating a wall hanging and liked how it turned out. I thought others would too and listed some for sale in my online shop. They sold wildly. So much so that the business completely evolved into faux floral designs.

Flowers in the form of faux floral wreaths found me when I didn't know I needed them. As time went on, I continued to hone my skills and develop my unique twist on wreath design. And I'm here to teach you how! I'm here to share that floral magic with you.

The starting point for all the projects in this book is the inspiration from nature itself: the woods, the garden and the field. What a gift it is that we can take nature's best from each of these places and add our own creative touch for our enjoyment!

Projects are divided seasonally and by skill level, so they can be made by anyone the whole year through. The materials used in all the projects, while artificial, closely resemble the real thing found in nature, giving these wreath designs a realistic, florist-quality look. And because these are artificial, you can enjoy your handiwork for years to come.

The great thing about using faux flowers is that you can start right where you are on a small scale and take your time. Most important, use this creative time for *you*. This is your chance to explore and expand your artistic side. Whether you are a seasoned maker looking to try a new medium or someone completely new to working with your hands, this is where you start. This is your time to work with flowers in a specific and approachable way, what so many people only wish they could do. And here you are, showing up and ready to begin. Happy creating!

Stephanie Petrak

one

Getting Ready
to Create a Wreath

Wreaths appeal to me because they are practical and endlessly creative. They provide a strong medium for creative expression that is completely useful after you're done creating. Wreaths are typically the first thing you see when entering your home, your own place in the big world, so why not make that entry beautiful and unique? I love the juxtaposition of the circular, confined base that can be opened up into a wild, unconfined shape with the addition of artistic materials. The strong sturdy base holds delicate, free-flowing flowers, a combination working together for a front door piece of art. You can make wreaths for the season, for the holiday or just because you like a certain flower. The possibilities are endless with wreaths.

Let's get started with all the supplies you will need for any wreath project.

Here is a side-by-side comparison of the two sizes of wreaths I recommend for hanging on a front door. To the left is the Large Wreath, and to the right is the Standard Wreath.

THE RIGHT WREATH BASE

The first step to wreath design is selecting your wreath base. As the foundation of a house is critical, so is the wreath base.

The wreath base used in the designs in this book is made of intertwined grapevine branches. I like using the grapevine bases for their natural feel, and also because the multiple branches give lots of space to hold more pieces in intricate designs.

The projects in this book list the size of grapevine base used, and the projects can be easily converted to whatever size you need.

Selecting the Right Size

Size for Front Doors

Consider your front door and entry as a whole. I have two size recommendations that will work well for any home:

Standard Wreath: Not large, not small and perfect for a regular-sized door about 35 to 36 inches (89 to 91 cm) across. The wreath base for this door is 14 inches (36 cm). The overall wreath size with greenery will vary depending on the shape of the wreath, anywhere from 19 to 26 inches (48 to 66 cm). The Standard Wreath is good for:

- Regular doors on small or medium homes
- Any size home with a lot of décor on the porch so as not to compete with additional décor
- Homes with double regular-sized front doors with a wreath on each door

Large Wreath: The next size up is a large wreath made on an 18 inch (46 cm) base with the overall size with greenery up to 30 inches or more (76+ cm). I would select this larger-sized wreath for:

- Doors larger than 36 inches (91 cm) across on larger homes
- Regular doors with window panels on either side, making the door appear larger
- Anyone who just likes big wreaths

Anything larger or smaller is purely based on your preference, which is totally fine too.

Size for Inside the Home

Selecting a wreath size for an interior space is subject to how and where you are using it. Will it be on an interior door, kitchen wall, gallery wall or somewhere else? Simply measure the space you want to fill, and that will be the overall target size.

Making the Base Project-Ready

Once you select the right size, choose a grapevine base that closely matches the shape indicated in your project. Some projects use a standard circular base while others utilize an oval-shaped base. Also, look for a base with the individual grapevine branches woven tightly together. Any gaps in the grapevine branches will make it harder to securely attach all the florals.

When you are ready to start your project, take a pair of wire cutters and trim off any trailing or unattached pieces from the grapevine base for a neat and easy-to-work-with base. Some grapevine bases may still have dried grapevine leaves in them. Pick out any loose or large clumps of leaves to expose as much of the branches as possible. Then, your base is ready to go!

A great wreath base has an even shape and grapevine branches woven tightly together. This will make creating your projects much easier and give better results.

Some grapevine bases have unruly twigs sticking out. Simply trim off these pieces with your wire cutters for a nice, even base.

My favorite faux flowers to use closely resemble what you would find in nature, in both color and texture.

SELECTING THE BEST FAUX FLORALS

Faux flowers have come a long way in terms of availability of selection and quality. I always seek out the highest quality in all that I do, and I have not been disappointed with what I can find at local craft stores and online stores in terms of faux flowers. My go-to places for purchasing my wreath-making supplies are Hobby Lobby, Michael's and AFloral (online at www.afloral.com).

Tacky faux flowers are a thing of the past. If you want to fill your home with beautiful blooms without the effort and expense of weekly fresh ones, faux is the way to go. When kept protected from weather elements like the sun, strong winds, rain and snow, your designs will last for years to come. Also, faux flowers are even more forgiving when it comes to designing than fresh ones. You can form them into the exact right shape for your project, fluff them and even trim leaves and petals off just like fresh flowers—all without water and the threat of them withering and shrinking.

Selecting the faux florals for a project is one of my favorite parts of the creative process. It's almost like a treasure hunt to find supplies that are just right. Here are some things to keep in mind to select the best faux flowers:

1. Use a variety of flowers or greenery that you would traditionally find in nature and in its natural colors.
2. When using materials made with fabric-like polyester, look for those with a softer feel where the fabric is tightly woven, thick and not fraying.
3. When using materials made of plastic, look for those with impressed details and more intricate shaping. These tend to not look like they are obviously made of plastic.
4. Use materials with variegated coloring as this more closely resembles the real thing.

My favorite types of faux stems to use in wreaths include:

1. Dahlias
2. Peonies
3. Open, ruffled roses
4. Eucalyptus
5. Ferns
6. Trailing vines

If you cannot find a specific material listed for your project, I suggest looking for something that closely matches both the color and size of what you can't find so it can seamlessly work with the other materials in the design. For example, if your project calls for a taupe rose but you can't seem to find one, a taupe peony or dahlia can do the trick. The same would apply to greenery.

Don't worry about finding tools that are pretty. Tools are utilitarian and help you get the job done.

TOOLS NEEDED

You will need some basic tools for all the projects included in this book:

Wire cutters

Because you will be cutting wired stems to size and trimming bushes, select the most heavy-duty wire cutters available at your craft store so you can trim through thicker stems without hurting your wrist.

Hot-glue gun for high-temperature glue and glue sticks

Unless otherwise indicated, all project materials included in this book are individually attached to the grapevine wreath base using high-temperature hot glue. High-temperature hot glue adheres the faux floral materials more securely than low-temperature glue. Craft stores sell both types—high-temperature–only glue guns as well as dual-temperature glue guns. Either type of glue gun will work well.

I prefer using a glue gun that accommodates the ⅝-inch (2-cm) glue sticks because a wreath project requires several glue sticks. Some glue guns can even accommodate extra-long glue sticks so you don't have to stop to refill nearly as often while you complete your project.

The glue gun will most likely drip when rested on a table, so place it on a paper plate or piece of cardboard to prevent any damage to your work surface. Obviously the high-temperature glue is very hot, so please be mindful of your hands and any drips off your materials as you work.

22-gauge floral wire

Some projects require materials such as garlands or fruit that are better secured to the wreath using floral wire. I like to use a thicker 22-gauge wire to match the sturdiness of the grapevine base. I also use this floral wire to make a simple wire loop for hanging the wreath.

HANGING YOUR COMPLETED DESIGN

Many different techniques are used in hanging a wreath depending on the hanging location and your personal preference. I suggest attaching a loop to the back of the wreath made of floral wire or twine for ease of use, but the wreath can be hung by just the grapevine branches alone too. Then the wreath can be hung in place in the following ways:

1. Over-the-door wreath hanger
2. Ribbon secured over the door either with a thumbtack to the top edge of the door, or to a hook attached to the top of the door on the inside
3. Common nail
4. Command strip hook (make sure to select one that will hold the weight of the wreath)
5. Wreath stand for displaying indoors on a mantel or table

Two

Wreath Design Foundational Techniques

I learned to design wreaths by just playing with them on my own. This has allowed me to develop approachable techniques to produce a lush wreath in a unique style. These techniques are essential to the whimsical projects found in this book. They ensure the wreath is wild yet balanced and use standard good design principles found across all creative disciplines. These techniques can be applied to any type of wreath you'd like to create.

TRIMMING MATERIALS

Trimming to Size

All faux floral materials listed in the projects include a "trimmed to size" length. This should always include leaving bare stem at the end of the material for attaching: at least 2 inches (5 cm) of bare stem for filler greenery and 4 inches (10 cm) of bare stem for blooms. This will leave plenty of stem to nestle into the wreath and grab hold of the grapevine base. You don't want these stems to fall out later! If you have any leaves or branches at the end of your cut stem, simply snip those off with your wire cutters.

Trimming by Type of Material

Stems—Stems are comprised of one main branch that has a flower blossom and/or a few individual branches coming off the main branch. Stems are the simplest to select and trim because you can clearly see their length. The multiple branches on a stem can be trimmed into individual pieces. Don't forget to leave enough stem to attach to the base, according to the lengths in the previous section.

Bushes—Whether of flowers or greenery, one bush can give you a multitude of individual stems. Bushes consist of multiple branches of the same flower or greenery. Be sure to look for bushes with several individual stems that can be trimmed to the adequate size of at least 2 inches (5 cm) of bare stem for attaching. Some bushes have leaf sets that can slide upward too, giving you a denser cluster of leaves and a longer stem. A good value for bushes is at least six individual stems on one bush.

Faux flowers are easier to attach to your project and position in the design when all of the leaves are removed from the stem.

Bushes are especially useful for filler greenery when you need several stems of the same variety.

I prefer to cut greenery garlands into individual pieces so I have more control of their use in a design.

Garlands—Sometimes the only adequate greenery you can find is in garland form, which is completely doable. Simply trim the garland itself into individual pieces to the correct size, and trim off any leaves to leave a bare stem for attaching.

DESIGN TECHNIQUES

The true mark of a high-quality wreath design is when it's full yet smooth in structure. I don't like designs that appear clumpy and uneven. That's why with every single piece I make, no matter how many times I've made it, I hang the wreath up somewhere or lay it on the ground and step back to see if there are any gaps that can be filled in and if the design is balanced in terms of focal flowers to accents and greenery. First look at the wreath as a whole and then look at the details to see if it's pleasing to the eye. To better achieve this, I use the following techniques when building my more traditional wreaths.

The Spiller Technique

The Spiller Technique begins several projects, like The Avondale on page 61. I think of this technique as forming a "greenery halo" around the outside of the wreath base that feathers away from the bulk of the wreath project.

1. To achieve this look, begin by trimming the Spiller Technique materials indicated in the project to size. These will be some of the longer pieces you'll be using.

2. Next, give the stems a little bend to follow a counterclockwise flow of the wreath.

3. Positioning the stems around the base first—before attaching—can help in evenly spacing everything. The exact spacing of all the Spiller Technique materials will be listed in each project, but usually the bases of the stems are secured around 4 to 7 inches (10 to 18 cm) apart. Attach each stem with hot glue on the outside edge of the wreath about 1 inch (3 cm) from the edge. Attach the stem so it lays parallel with the grapevine base, slightly flowing out and away from the base.

The Filler Technique

The Filler Technique is used to begin evenly covering the grapevine base and avoid clumps right from the beginning, like in the Aria project on page 67. The filler greeneries used in this technique tend to be bushier, with smaller, full leaves.

For the filler, you will use one or two types of greenery, depending on what's listed for your selected project. The technique is the same for either but with one difference: When using two types of greenery, you will leave more space between the first greenery branches so the second type of greenery can fill in those gaps. This will be indicated in the project.

The filler greenery may range in size from just 4 inches (10 cm) long to upward of 8 inches (20 cm), depending on your material. I would keep the filler greenery to this size range for the best results. You want to execute the Filler Technique so that the grapevine wreath base is covered, but not so that the greenery is densely packed together.

The Filler Technique uses a basic zig-zag pattern when attaching the greenery.

1. To begin achieving that smooth, full base, first trim all the pieces you will need to size so you have a large pile of ready-to-go pieces.
2. Take your first piece of greenery and attach it with hot glue to the center edge of the grapevine base.
3. Take another piece of the same greenery, layering slightly with the piece you already attached. Glue this piece near the outer edge of the wreath. When using two greeneries, you will leave a larger gap as you repeat the pattern, otherwise attach the next piece back at the center edge again, filling in near the attached greeneries.
4. Continue this zig-zag pattern until you've reached all around the grapevine base.
5. If you are using two greeneries, repeat the same process again with the second type of greenery, filling in the gaps.

The Focal Trio Technique

Groups of three elements are pleasing to the eye. When using multiple flowers in a wreath, I like to use the Focal Trio Technique, which is simply nestling three flowers together in a triangle shape to form one large bunch, like in the Florio project on page 53. When creating a large swath of flowers with many blooms, use multiple Focal Trios connected by one or two other flowers to create an even look.

Now that you've learned the foundations of excellent faux floral wreath design, let's dive into some projects to practice and use these design skills. These projects focus on mastering the foundational techniques you've learned so that they will eventually become second nature to you in your creative journey. Let these design principles guide you, but also trust your instincts, even in the beginning. As you let yourself create, you will develop your own style, trust your ideas more and be able to create fearlessly.

PROJECT SKILL LEVELS

Whether you are creating a wreath for the first time or looking to further your crafting handiwork, each project is marked with a skill level to meet you where you are.

BEGINNER

· Uses foundational techniques outlined above
· Classic, easy-to-find color palettes
· Manageable variety of supplies
· Easy design shape

INTERMEDIATE

· Builds off the Beginner skill level by playing with more interesting shapes
· Requires a more precise placement of materials

ADVANCED

· Focuses on complex shape and movement
· Includes several accent pieces
· More sophisticated color palettes
· More steps to complete the project

three

From the Garden

My garden is my refuge in the summertime, allowing me to watch the progress of everything growing and smell the sweetness of the floral season. A stroll through the garden in its purposely placed rows feels like a breath of fresh air. This chapter features floral-focused designs and all the pretty blooms we find in the garden.

Gardens begin in the spring and last through the fall, giving an abundance of colorful blooms ready for you in all shapes, colors and sizes. Capture the magic of the growing season and bring it into your creative wreath designs, which are easy to achieve with life-like artificial blooms readily available for crafters. These wreath designs are a bit more on the traditional side with a whimsical twist and lots of flowers, like in The Avondale (page 61) design featuring an abundance of dahlias or The Adelaide (page 41) wreath bursting with pink roses. A lush greenery base helps the stellar garden blooms stand out.

the Wedgemere

SEASON: Year Round

SKILL LEVEL: Beginner

FINISHED SIZE: Up to 26" (66 cm) with greenery

An herb wreath is a classic choice for a wreath design, but the shape of what is traditionally seen is basically the same everywhere: sections of herbs all around the wreath. While that's all fine and good, I like to take what is expected and make it unconfined and different. This Wedgemere project lets the herbs move a lot more and they are used in a modern shape. The full variety of herbs may be harder to come by in-store, but they are readily available through online retailers.

TOOLS

Grapevine wreath base (14" [36 cm])

Wire cutters

High-temperature hot-glue gun and glue sticks (all materials are attached using hot glue unless otherwise specified)

TRIMMED MATERIALS

3 large basil sprays (13" [33 cm])

2 small mint sprays (9" [23 cm])

3 small purple sage sprays (9" [23 cm])

3 small rosemary bushes (10" [25 cm])

4 woodsy leafy branches (12" [30 cm])

START WITH THE BASE

1. Begin the herb base by attaching one large basil spray on the right side of the wreath in the middle going upward, and then use another spray to mirror the top spray going down, leaving a gap of about 7 inches (18 cm) between the sprays.

2. Layer the small mint sprays on the large basil sprays using the same technique by attaching one above and one below to form a closed center. Fluff and spread the small mint spray leaves.

3. Layer the small purple sage around the small mint sprays by attaching one top right, one to the left of the lower mint leaves and one bottom right. Spread the leaves out.

4. Use the small rosemary bushes to layer around the small mint sprays and small purple sage sprays by attaching one on the top left, one bottom center and one center right, extending straight out. Fluff and spread out the branches.

MAKE IT INTERESTING WITH ACCENTS

5. Attach the woodsy leafy branches around the herbs to give the wreath a larger, more dramatic shape—two flanking the top large basil spray, one bottom right directed straight down and another on the bottom left following the curve of the wreath base.

FINISH THE WREATH

6. Tuck the last large basil spray into the bottom left small rosemary spray and bend following the inside curve of the grapevine wreath base to finish your Wedgemere wreath.

To hang your new wreath, see page 17 for ideas.

the Piper

SEASON: Year Round

SKILL LEVEL: Beginner

FINISHED SIZE: Up to 23" (58 cm) with greenery

Anemones are one of the flowers I used in my very first faux floral arrangement.
I was drawn to them right from the beginning partly because I am biased to the classic black
and white color combination, but I also think the black center atop the crisp white floral
petals are even more stunning when paired with greenery. It's a visual party of color contrasts.
Given that the anemones are so visually striking, this Piper design also includes the oh-so-soft
dusty miller to balance the strength of the anemones. Fresh, simple greenery provides
the perfect base to this duo of soft and strong.

TOOLS

Grapevine wreath base (14" [36 cm])

Wire cutters

High-temperature hot-glue gun and glue sticks (all materials are attached
using hot glue unless otherwise specified)

TRIMMED MATERIALS

10 dark leafy greenery branches (11" [28 cm])

14 light greenery branches (9" [23 cm])

14 dusty miller branches (6" [15 cm])

5 white anemones (5" [13-cm] blooms)

3 white rose sprays (2" [5-cm] blooms)

10 rosemary branches (7" [18 cm])

10 flowering heather branches (10" [25 cm])

START WITH THE BASE

1. Attach the dark leafy greenery branches to the grapevine wreath base using the Spiller Technique (page 23), about 4 inches (10 cm) apart.

2. Using the Filler Technique (page 24), attach ten of the light greenery branches to the center of the grapevine wreath base, leaving space for the dusty miller branches, reserving four light greenery branches for step 8.

ADD THE FLORALS

3. Fill in the remaining space between the ten light greenery branches on the grapevine wreath base with ten of the dusty miller branches using the Filler Technique (page 24), reserving four dusty miller branches for step 8.

4. Attach the white anemones around the wreath, not perfectly spaced out. Try placing a pair of white anemones closer together and leave one by itself, making sure the space between the flowers is balanced. Leave the floral heads suspended just over the greenery base and not tucked into the greenery.

5. Nestle and attach the white rose sprays with the anemones, scattered around the wreath.

MAKE IT INTERESTING WITH ACCENTS

6. Attach seven of the rosemary branches to the outside edge of the wreath, spiraling outward in the counterclockwise direction of the greenery. Do the same for the inside edge of the wreath with the three remaining rosemary branches, giving the rosemary branches a bit of a bend before attaching.

7. Attach five of the flowering heather branches between the anemone flowers on the center part of the wreath, flowing outward with the greenery. Then, attach the remaining five flowering heather branches evenly spaced along the outside edge of the wreath.

8. Finish your beautiful new Piper wreath by checking for evenness of greenery along the outer edge of the wreath. Use the remaining four light greenery branches and four dusty miller branches to fill in the outside edge of the wreath as needed.

To hang your new wreath, see page 17 for ideas.

The Adelaide

SEASON: Spring

SKILL LEVEL: Advanced

FINISHED SIZE: Up to 24" (61 cm) with greenery

The shabby chic style inspiration for this wreath comes straight from a cottage garden, with classic pink roses. High-quality and interesting roses are easy to find and incorporate into wreath designs. For this project, I like to use rose sprays, which consist of multiple rose blooms on one stem. The blooms on the rose sprays vary in how open they are, ranging from a closed bud to a fully bloomed flower, giving a true from-the-garden feel. Adding to the soft feel of this design are fuzzy lamb's ears and delicate white heather, all grounded with rose leaves and boxwood stems.

TOOLS

Grapevine wreath base (14" [36 cm])

Wire cutters

High-temperature hot-glue gun and glue sticks (all materials are attached using hot glue unless otherwise specified)

TRIMMED MATERIALS

12 pink wildflower and greenery stems (12" [30 cm])

12 boxwood branches (11" [28 cm])

12 rose leaves branches (10" [25 cm])

4 pink rose sprays (3.5" [9-cm] blooms)

6 lightest pink roses (2–3" [5–8-cm] blooms)

3 mini pink wild rose stems (9" [23 cm])

4 lamb's ear stems (15" [38 cm])

8 white heather branches (15" [38 cm])

START WITH THE BASE

1. Attach eight of the pink wildflower and greenery stems to the grapevine wreath base using the Spiller Technique (page 23), about 5 inches (13 cm) apart, reserving four for step 7.

2. Attach the boxwood branches to the center of the grapevine wreath base using the Filler Technique (page 24), leaving space for the rose leaves branches.

3. Fill in the remaining space between the boxwood branches on the grapevine wreath base with the rose leaves branches using the Filler Technique (page 24).

ADD THE FLORALS

4. Attach the pink rose sprays and lightest pink roses to the wreath on the right side, alternating pink and lightest pink roses, leaving some space for the greenery to show through the floral cluster.

5. Attach the mini pink wild rose stems tucked into the cluster of roses, one on the top, one on the right side and one on the bottom.

MAKE IT INTERESTING WITH ACCENTS

6. Attach the lamb's ear stems on the top, bottom and right side of the roses, evenly spaced along the right side of the wreath.

7. Use the remaining four pieces of the pink wildflower and greenery stems to tuck into the center greenery part of the wreath, evenly spacing from where the roses begin and end.

8. Use three of the white heather branches to also tuck into the center greenery, between the pink wildflower and greenery stems.

FINISH THE WREATH

9. Use the remaining white heather branches to finish the wreath by accenting the roses. Add five individual stems all around the roses on the outside edge between the lamb's ear stems, evenly spaced from top to bottom.

To hang your new wreath, see page 17 for ideas.

The Eccleston

SEASON: Year Round

SKILL LEVEL: Advanced

FINISHED SIZE: Up to 38" (97 cm) with astilbe reaching farther

If you're feeling adventurous and have a large space to decorate, such as above a fireplace, on a porch wall or in an event space, I invite you to the fun of an extra-large statement wreath like this Eccleston project. The great thing about these stunning pieces is that even though they are much larger than front door wreaths, they use the same techniques, just on a grander scale. Adding florals to a large design gives the wreath an even more stunning impact. Several full hydrangea blooms—my favorite flowers—work well with the extra-large size.

TOOLS

Grapevine wreath base (24" [61 cm])

Wire cutters

High-temperature hot-glue gun and glue sticks (all materials are attached using hot glue unless otherwise specified)

TRIMMED MATERIALS

12 button leaf branches (12" [30 cm])

18 mini ferns (12" [30 cm])

18 silver-dollar eucalyptus stems (12" [30 cm])

3 large cream hydrangeas (7" [18-cm] blooms)

3 taupe peonies (6" [15-cm] blooms)

3 taupe dahlias (5" [13-cm] blooms)

6 creamy white roses (3" [8-cm] blooms)

4 blush peonies (3" [8-cm] blooms)

6 astilbe sprays (18" [46 cm])

5 green hypericum berry stems (13" [33 cm])

6 long and 3 short hanging leafy branches (15" [38 cm] and 10" [25 cm])

BEGIN WITH THE BASE

1. Use the Spiller Technique (page 23) to evenly space the button leaf branches around the outside edge of the grapevine wreath base. Attach the button leaf branches 6 inches (15 cm) apart but with the branches bent close together.

2. Use the Filler Technique (page 24) to attach the mini ferns all around the wreath, leaving space for the silver-dollar eucalyptus stems.

3. Use the Filler Technique (page 24) to attach the silver-dollar eucalyptus stems in the gaps among the mini ferns.

ADD THE FLORALS

4. For the florals, you will create three Focal Trios (page 26) each consisting of one large cream hydrangea, one taupe peony and one taupe dahlia. Attach the first Focal Trio in the upper-right section of the wreath. Next, attach the second focal trio in the center-right section of the wreath. Attach the final Focal Trio in the bottom-center section of the wreath. The Focal Trios should have about 4 inches (10 cm), or the width of a floral blossom, between them.

5. Use the creamy white roses and the blush peonies as accent blooms to scatter around the wreath. Begin by adding one blush peony and one creamy white rose between the top Focal Trio and center Focal Trio to connect them. Next, add one creamy white rose between the center Focal Trio and bottom Focal Trio. Finally, evenly scatter to your liking the remaining blush peonies and creamy white roses around the greenery part of the wreath to complete the circle of florals in the wreath.

MAKE IT INTERESTING WITH ACCENTS

6. Attach the astilbe sprays as accents to the main florals on the right side of the wreath. Attach two astilbe sprays right next to each other to form one piece directly above the top Focal Trio pointing upward. Next, attach another two astilbe sprays adjacent to the center Focal Trio pointing outward. Finally, attach the last two astilbe sprays on the bottom of the wreath in line with the top astilbe sprays, pointing downward.

7. Attach the green hypericum berry stems along the outside edge of the main swath of flowers and flanking the astilbe sprays.

FINISH THE WREATH

8. Use the hanging leafy branches as a final flowy finish to the wreath. Beginning with the long hanging leafy branches, attach one piece to the bottom center of the wreath. Use two more pieces on either side of the center astilbe sprays. Attach one more long hanging leafy branch to the top center of the wreath.

9. Use the three short hanging leafy branches to tuck into the left side of the wreath between the flowers in the center of the wreath to finish the Eccleston design.

To hang your new wreath, see page 17 for ideas.

the Florio

SEASON: Summer

SKILL LEVEL: Beginner

FINISHED SIZE: Up to 26" (66 cm) with greenery

If you're looking to have fun with color in your design, the technique to try is ombré. Creating an ombré effect in a wreath will challenge you to really focus on color and notice the beautifully subtle nuances between shades. If the thought of selecting all these flowing colors is intimidating, find one flower in a color you love, and build the ombré effect from that color.

TOOLS

Grapevine wreath base (14" [36 cm])

Wire cutters

High-temperature hot-glue gun and glue sticks (all materials are attached using hot glue unless otherwise specified)

TRIMMED MATERIALS

7 long and 3 short variegated fern branches (13" [33 cm] and 9" [23 cm])

18 mini ferns (8" [20 cm])

1 ivory rose (5" [3-cm] bloom)

2 ivory with hints of pink peonies (6" [15-cm] blooms)

1 medium pink dahlia (6" [15-cm] bloom)

2 medium pink small floral branches (10" [25 cm])

1 hot pink rose (3.5" [9-cm] bloom)

2 dark pink carnations (4" [10-cm] blooms)

2 long and 3 short variegated leaf branches (16" [41 cm] and 7" [18 cm])

BEGIN WITH THE BASE

1. Attach the long variegated fern branches to the edge of the grapevine wreath base using the Spiller Technique (page 23) 6 inches (15 cm) apart but bent close together.

2. Using the Filler Technique (page 24), attach the mini ferns to the center of the grapevine wreath base.

ADD THE FLORALS

3. Create a Focal Trio (page 26) using the ivory rose on the bottom and the two ivory with hints of pink peonies on top. Attach these florals to the bottom right of the wreath.

4. Attach the medium pink dahlia above the ivory with hints of pink peonies.

5. Nestle in and attach the two medium pink small floral branches on either side of the medium pink dahlia.

6. Attach the hot pink rose above and to the right of the medium pink dahlia.

7. Attach one of the dark pink carnations next to the hot pink rose to form another Focal Trio (page 26) with the medium pink dahlia.

8. Attach the second dark pink carnation above and centered on the existing blooms.

9. Attach the three short variegated leaf branches to the center of the wreath among the mini ferns, evenly spacing out where you attach them, about 4 inches (10 cm) apart.

FINISH THE WREATH

10. Add the three short variegated fern branches to the center of the wreath between the variegated leaf stems, tucking them under the main florals if necessary.

11. To finish the Florio design, attach one long variegated leaf branch directly above the florals and the other directly below. Give the stems a little bend for more shape and a natural look.

To hang your new wreath, see page 17 for ideas.

$\mathscr{The}$ Avondale

SEASON: **Summer**

SKILL LEVEL: **Beginner**

FINISHED SIZE: **Up to 27" (69 cm) with greenery**

Dahlias are stately summer blooms loved for their vibrant colors and structured petals.
In an avid gardener's plot, you will find a row dedicated to just these profusely blooming
flowers. When you get a bunch of dahlia plants together, you create a swath of tall lush
greenery peppered with richly colored blooms. This swath of dahlias found in gardens and
farms is exactly what I wanted to re-create in this Avondale wreath. I chose the ball dahlia for
this project because of the large ball-shaped bloom made up of many perfectly formed petals.
Take a moment to really look at the structure of this bloom—it's truly fascinating!

TOOLS

Grapevine wreath base (18" [46 cm])

Wire cutters

High-temperature hot-glue gun and glue sticks (all materials are attached
using hot glue unless otherwise specified)

TRIMMED MATERIALS

9 delicate fern branches (10–12" [25–30 cm])

13 boxwood branches (11" [28 cm])

12 cream and pink variegated ball dahlia sprays with a bud (4" [10-cm] blooms)

8 pink viburnum sprays with leaves (11" [28 cm])

START WITH THE BASE

1. Attach the delicate fern branches to the grapevine wreath base using the Spiller Technique (page 23), with the tips spaced about 3 inches (8 cm) apart.

2. Use nine of the boxwood branches to evenly cover the entire grapevine wreath base, overlapping each other slightly, reserving the remaining four branches for step 8.

3

4

ADD THE FLORALS

3. Trim the buds off the cream and pink variegated ball dahlia sprays, then trim both the buds and blooms to size and reserve the buds for step 7. Begin adding the ball dahlias by first attaching four blooms: one each on the top, bottom, right and left sides of the wreath.

4. Then, create clusters of three cream and pink variegated ball dahlias around the first four cream and pink variegated ball dahlias. You don't want the cream and pink variegated ball dahlias perfectly aligned, so vary the positioning of the cream and pink variegated dahlias to create a whimsical flow of flowers around the wreath.

MAKE IT INTERESTING WITH ACCENTS

5. Attach four pieces of the pink viburnum sprays with leaves, one between each cluster of ball dahlias, following the flow of the wreath.

6. Attach the remaining four pink viburnum sprays with leaves, one on the outside edge of each cluster of ball dahlias.

7. Attach all the reserved cream and pink variegated ball dahlia buds among the dahlia clusters on the outside edge of the wreath, one bud for each blossom. Bend the buds to give them a more natural curving shape.

FINISH THE WREATH

8. Finish the Avondale wreath by filling in any gaps in the center circle of the wreath with the remaining four boxwood branches.

To hang your new wreath, see page 17 for ideas.

Aria

SEASON: Fall

SKILL LEVEL: Beginner

FINISHED SIZE: Up to 23" (58 cm) with greenery

A fall wreath doesn't have to include the colors red, orange and yellow to be seasonal. Neutral-toned florals paired with robust greenery and the delicate accent colors of the season make for a subtly fall décor piece. This Aria design uses ivory, tan and brown florals with dusty pink berries to provide that hint of fall. The wreath is so neutral, you could get away with hanging it year round, too.

TOOLS

Grapevine wreath base (14" [36 cm])

Wire cutters

High-temperature hot-glue gun and glue sticks (all materials are attached using hot glue unless otherwise specified)

TRIMMED MATERIALS

27 feathery ferns (10" [25 cm])

15 blossoming grasses (8" [20 cm])

15 blue-gray silver-dollar eucalyptus branches (8" [20 cm])

1 large brown dahlia (6" [15-cm] bloom)

1 ivory rose (5" [13-cm] bloom)

6 caramel magnolias with leaves (4" [10-cm] blooms)

7 dusty pink berry clusters (5" [13 cm])

START WITH THE BASE

1. Begin the base of the wreath by attaching the feathery ferns using the Spiller Technique (page 23) all around the grapevine wreath base. You will want these pieces attached close together, about 2 inches (5 cm) apart at the base.

2. Use the Filler Technique (page 24) to attach nine pieces of the blossoming grasses, leaving some space for the silver-dollar eucalyptus branches, saving the six remaining blossoming grasses for step 8.

3. Attach nine pieces of the silver-dollar eucalyptus branches using the Filler Technique (page 24) to fill in the gaps of the grapevine wreath base, saving the six remaining branches for step 8.

ADD THE FLORALS

4. Attach the large brown dahlia on the bottom-right side of the wreath.

5. Attach the ivory rose to the top-left side of the wreath, diagonally across from the large brown dahlia.

6. Scatter and attach the six caramel magnolias with leaves around the wreath, positioning some closer than others.

7. Evenly scatter and nestle the dusty pink berry clusters among the flowers all around the wreath.

FINISH THE WREATH

8. Finish your Aria wreath by adding the remaining silver-dollar eucalyptus branches and blossoming grasses around the outside edge of the wreath to fill in any gaps or to break up large clumps of one color.

To hang your new wreath, see page 17 for ideas.

The Blomfield

SEASON: Fall

SKILL LEVEL: Beginner

FINISHED SIZE: Up to 21" (53 cm) across and 32" (82 cm) long with greenery

Majestic sunflowers are a staple for the fall season, but I wanted to use these traditional yellow blooms in a new way by giving them some fun accent colors. This Blomfield design highlights the sunflowers by using purple leaves and adding a pop of color with some magenta mini flowering branches. This design also has a modern shape, leaving some of the grapevine wreath base exposed to modernize the sunflowers.

TOOLS

Grapevine wreath base (14" [36 cm])

Wire cutters

High-temperature hot-glue gun and glue sticks (all materials are attached using hot glue unless otherwise specified)

TRIMMED MATERIALS

25 neutral green eucalyptus branches (10" [25 cm])

9 sunflowers (3–4" [8–10-cm] blooms)

5 purple leaf branches (9" [23 cm])

5 magenta mini flowering branches (20" [51 cm])

START WITH THE BASE

1. To provide a light base for the sunflowers, begin by attaching six pieces of the neutral green eucalyptus branches on the right side of the grapevine wreath base, saving the nineteen remaining branches for steps 5 and 6. Place the six pieces into two groups of three coming from the center of the grapevine wreath base, one set of three going upward and the other set going downward, leaving about 2 inches (5 cm) of space between the two groups on the grapevine wreath base.

ADD THE FLORALS

2. Attach the sunflowers to the right side of the wreath among the eucalyptus base to create an even swath of blooms. You can achieve this by making several Focal Trios (page 26) of sunflower blossoms and connecting these groups with a single sunflower where needed.

MAKE IT INTERESTING WITH ACCENTS

3. Tuck two purple leaf branches behind the sunflowers, one at the top and one at the bottom, curving with the shape of the wreath. Attach the three remaining purple leaf branches on the right side of the sunflowers pointing outward.

4. Use the magenta mini flowering branches to give the wreath a more whimsical shape by attaching two branches at the top of the wreath and three flowing from the bottom.

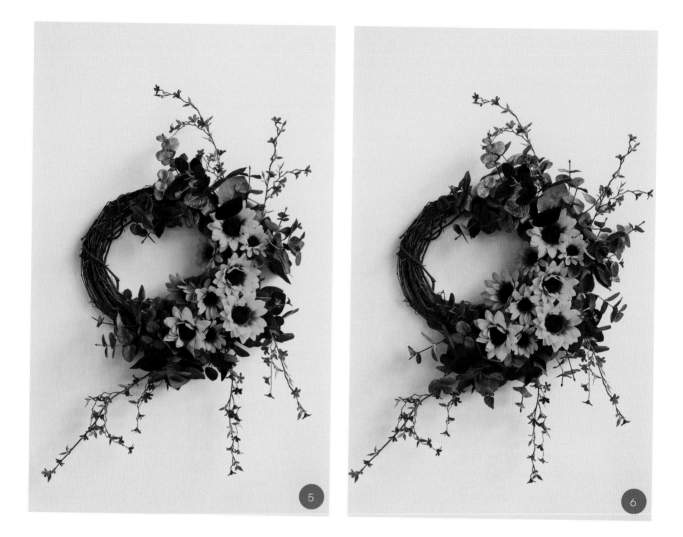

FINISH THE WREATH

5. Finish your beautiful new Blomfield wreath by filling in the outside edge of the design with six of the remaining neutral green eucalyptus branches. Use three pieces flanking the purple leaf branches on the top, flowing with the grapevine wreath base, and three pieces also flanking the purple leaf branches on the bottom, flowing with the grapevine wreath base as well.

6. Use the remaining neutral green eucalyptus branches to fill in along the right side of the wreath, allowing some of the ends to stick out.

To hang your new wreath, see page 17 for ideas.

four

From the Woods

Mysterious, quiet, alone, peaceful, majestic: These are words that come to mind when I think of hiking through the woods. We go to the woods for solitude and to find quiet again. We go to be grounded on this earth in its raw natural beauty. In the chaos of everyday life, we can find peace in the woods. The woods serve as a perfect inspiration for wreaths to be hung in our homes, bringing that peace indoors.

The projects in this chapter take the best materials found in the woods and highlight their mystery and grandeur by using strong shape and design. The following designs use these elements to step out of the traditional circular wreath shape for a wilder look. This look is achieved by using woodsy branches spinning off the grapevine wreath base in a purposeful, design-focused way, like in The Cecily (page 91) and The Sulina (page 95). Ferns, tree branches and moss are wonderful natural elements to bring that rustic nature feel to your home décor.

the Kinley

SEASON: Year Round

SKILL LEVEL: Advanced

FINISHED SIZE: Up to 30" (76 cm) across with greenery

This Kinley wreath design focuses on ferns and all their lovely color variations, sizes and shapes. This design utilizes a mix of different ferns for a medley of woodsy greenery that's perfect for decorating your home all year long. Ferns are so ubiquitous and are a strong staple to the wooded ground cover. When searching for the fern varieties used in this design, look for both color variances and shape variances to provide the eye a pleasing mixture. Look for dark and light colors in straight, ruffled or round shapes. Most important, find what you like and use it!

TOOLS

Oval grapevine wreath base (18" [46 cm])

Wire cutters

High-temperature hot-glue gun and glue sticks (all materials are attached using hot glue unless otherwise specified)

TRIMMED MATERIALS

12 dark ferns with thin leaves (12–14" [30–36 cm] long)

9 light sage ferns (13" [33 cm] long)

6 large and 3 small dark ferns with thick leaves (13" [33 cm] and 8" [20 cm] long)

START WITH THE BASE

1. Orient the oval grapevine wreath base vertically. The focal point of this design will be the bottom-center of the wreath. Attach the dark ferns with thin leaves to the oval grapevine wreath base to begin the base shape of the wreath. Attach five on the left side of the focal point and seven on the right, spaced out about 6 inches (15 cm) apart and flowing outward and upward from the base. Give the stems a good bend in varying directions to create flow.

FILL THE WREATH

2. Use the light sage fern pieces to fill in the wreath. Begin at the center focal point and attach six coming out from that point: three from the left and three from the right, fanning out from that center focal point.

3. Attach an additional light sage fern up the left side of the wreath and then two more up the right side of the wreath. The tips should end short of the base of the dark ferns with thin leaves pieces.

FINISH THE WREATH

4. Finish the center focal point with the three small dark ferns with thick leaves pieces by tucking them into the light sage fern, going to the left, right and downward. Mix the branches of the dark ferns with thick leaves and light sage fern together a little bit to blend.

5. Attach the six large dark ferns with thick leaves pieces to finish the shape of the wreath. For the left side, attach one on the bottom-outside edge bending outward, one tucked into the middle section and one straight on top. Repeat for the right side: Attach one on the bottom bending outward, one in the middle section and one on top. Be sure to place the ferns where there may be a gap in the shape and give them a slight bend for a more natural look to complete the Kinley design.

To hang your new wreath, see page 17 for ideas.

the Penley

SKILL LEVEL: Advanced

FINISHED SIZE: Up to 23" (58 cm) with trailing greenery extending an additional 7" (18 cm)

On a walk in the park or even in your own backyard, you will probably find woodsy and shade-loving moss. Known to grow on the north side of trees and stones, moss is a wonderful natural element to add to your wreaths with its low profile and soft texture. Most moss in craft stores isn't technically artificial but rather dried. I still like to sneak some into my artificial designs. Add some moss as the last step when your design is nearly complete as moss is delicate and will fall apart if handled too much, so work gingerly. In this design, the dragon ferns contrast nicely with the soft moss and light-colored florals. The ferns provide an anchor to the overall design, giving the wreath a defined shape and strong movement.

TOOLS

Grapevine wreath base (14" [36 cm])

5 pieces of 22-gauge floral wire (8" [20 cm])

Wire cutters

High-temperature hot-glue gun and glue sticks (all materials are attached using hot glue unless otherwise specified)

TRIMMED MATERIALS

Mossy garland (you want something similar to Spanish moss and artificial for this part; 6' [2 m] long)

1 ivory hydrangea (7" [18-cm] bloom)

1 large light purple dahlia (7" [18-cm] bloom)

1 deep purple rose (3" [8-cm] bloom with optional buds)

2 pink sedum stems (7" [18 cm])

3 dragon fern stems (17" [43 cm])

5 long and 3 short dark maple leaf branches (11–14" [28–36 cm] and 9" [23 cm] long)

4 wispy accent ferns (12" [30 cm])

2 mini white flower stems (9" [23 cm])

Light green moss (1 package, around 100 cubic inches)

START WITH THE BASE

1. Use the mossy garland to line the inside center of the grapevine wreath base; trim to size. Take the remaining garland and line the outside rim of the wreath. The garland may not completely cover the grapevine wreath, but the florals will cover any exposed grapevine. Use a piece of floral wire to wrap around the grapevine wreath base to secure to the base about every 5 inches (13 cm).

ADD THE FLORALS

2. Using the Focal Trio Technique (page 26), attach the ivory hydrangea, large light purple dahlia and deep purple rose to the wreath where the grapevine may still be exposed, centered on the right side of the wreath: hydrangea first front and center, dahlia on top of the hydrangea slightly to the right and finally the rose on top to the left.

3. Nestle the pink sedum stems beside the florals and attach one cluster on top of the florals and one on the bottom.

4. Take the dragon fern stems and form them into organic "S" shapes. Attach them on the outside edge of the grapevine base with one fern directly above the florals, one directly below the florals and one to the bottom right.

5.   Attach the five long dark maple leaf branches surrounding the dragon fern stems, filling in any gaps between these elements.

6.   Use the three short dark maple leaf branches and attach them to the center of the wreath in the mossy garland, evenly spacing them out where you attach them, about 4 inches (10 cm) apart.

7. Tuck and attach the four stems of wispy accent ferns evenly spaced out among the maple leaves and dragon ferns.

8. Using the two mini white flower stems, simply nestle and attach them below the Focal Trio of flowers.

9. To finish The Penley, hot glue clusters of light green moss directly on the florals and greenery all around the wreath, making sure the green color is evenly distributed around the wreath. Use varying size moss clusters for even more texture and interest. To make a larger moss cluster, simply hot glue a few individual pieces on top of each other until you get the right size.

To hang your new wreath, see page 17 for ideas.

the Cecily

SEASON: Spring

SKILL LEVEL: Intermediate

FINISHED SIZE: Up to 21" (53 cm) across and 40" (102 cm) tall with branches

Because winter is so long where I live in northeast Ohio, I get excited to see the first blooming branches on the trees and the greening and budding of perennial bushes. The blooms on flowering cherry trees are a beautiful and fragrant welcome to the new season. Thankfully, craft stores have tall, realistic artificial flowering branches to create wreath designs with epic shape. Branches are perfect to achieve this unconfined design as they are very structural and hold shape well. The strong branches are filled in and softened in this project with spring-green leafy branches, bringing that fresh feeling to your home.

TOOLS

Grapevine wreath base (14" [41 cm])

Wire cutters

High-temperature hot-glue gun and glue sticks (all materials are attached
using hot glue unless otherwise specified)

TRIMMED MATERIALS

2 pink cherry blossom branches (18" [46 cm])

3 ivory cherry blossom branches (18" [46 cm])

6 budding branches with leaves (8" [20 cm])

6 dogwood branches (12" [30 cm])

12 spring-green leafy branches (10" [25 cm])

START WITH THE BASE

1. Spread the individual branches on each main branch of the pink cherry blossom and ivory cherry blossom, and bend slightly to give them a realistic look. The stems should not be completely straight. You can also adjust the shape of the branches further once they are secured to the grapevine wreath base. Attach the two pink cherry blossom branches on the right side of the grapevine wreath base, from the center, with one branch flowing upward and the other flowing downward.

2. Attach the ivory cherry blossom branches adjacent to the pink cherry blossom branches, this time one on the top left of the pink cherry blossom flowing upward, one on the top right and the other on the bottom left of the pink cherry blossom branch flowing downward and slightly following the curve of the grapevine wreath base.

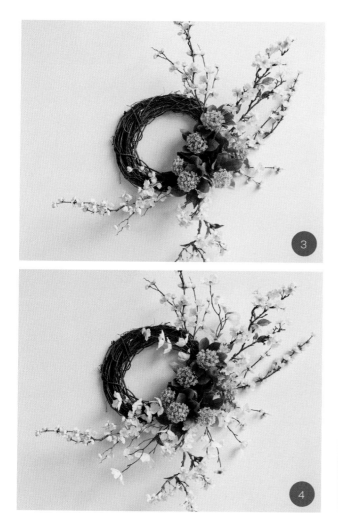

MAKE IT INTERESTING WITH ACCENTS

3. All six of the budding branches with leaves will provide the focal point of the wreath and will be secured in the center of where the cherry blossom branches meet on the grapevine wreath base. Attach the budding branches one by one, tucking each one into the next in varying directions so you form one group of buds, like a bush.

4. Add the six dogwood branches evenly scattered around the budding branches, tucking them into the leaves.

FINISH THE WREATH

5. Complete your Cecily wreath by filling in the gaps with the spring-green leafy branches. Attach the branches behind the ivory and pink cherry blossom branches. Continue to add the branches all around the outside of the wreath and budding focal point, filling in in any gaps and feathering out the design.

To hang your new wreath, see page 17 for ideas.

Sulina

SEASON: Fall

SKILL LEVEL: Intermediate

FINISHED SIZE: Up to 24" (61 cm) across and 38" (97 cm) long with greenery

My favorite type of wreath is overflowing with leafy branches. Something about the lushness is so comforting and relaxing. It feels like I am right in nature. This wreath takes all the majesty that is the fall-colored leaves and brings them to your front door. This design uses a variety of fall foliage in orange, yellow and green-brown tones in an interesting cascading shape, so you are whisked away in its flowing leaves in the crisp autumn breeze.

TOOLS

Oval grapevine wreath base (14" [36 cm]). Note: This is a perfect opportunity to use any more gnarly grapevine wreath bases you may come across, as the more twiggy, rough base fits well for this fall design.

Wire cutters

High-temperature hot-glue gun and glue sticks (all materials are attached using hot glue unless otherwise specified)

TRIMMED MATERIALS

5 weeping birch leaf branches (1.5–2' [46–61 cm])

12 fall oak leaf branches (14" [36 cm])

6 feathery fall grasses (12" [30 cm])

7 copper silver-dollar sprays (11" [28 cm])

START WITH THE BASE

1. Orient the oval grapevine wreath base vertically. Begin with the weeping birch leaf branches by attaching them individually to the grapevine wreath base, starting at the top center and evenly spacing the branches down the left side of the wreath to the bottom center, with all the branches hanging counterclockwise, following the shape of the grapevine wreath base. You want a consistent flow of leaves, with the bottom branch trailing off very long.

FILL THE WREATH

2. Bend the fall oak leaf branches to give them a natural, slightly curved shape. Use these branches to fill in the left side of the wreath, starting at the top where the weeping birch leaf branches begin and following the shape of the wreath down to where the bottom weeping birch branch trails off the grapevine wreath base.

3. Fill out and soften the edges of the wreath with the feathery fall grasses. Attach one feathery fall grass in the center of the wreath at the top where the weeping birch leaf branches begin, and attach another feathery fall grass where the weeping birch leaf branches end on the bottom of the wreath. Then, fill any gaps between the foliage you have attached on the outside edge of the wreath by attaching the remaining feathery fall grasses there. Be sure to have some feathery fall grasses extend out of the wreath so their lovely texture is seen.

FINISH THE WREATH

4. Finish The Sulina by evenly spreading the copper silver-dollar sprays all around the wreath. These branches should be peeking out of the foliage to give some dimension to the wreath and show off their stunning copper color, about 6 inches (15 cm) apart.

To hang your new wreath, see page 17 for ideas.

the Hollycroft

SEASON: Winter

SKILL LEVEL: Beginner

FINISHED SIZE: Up to 22" (56 cm) with greenery

For my holiday wreaths, I like to keep them very traditional, using nature-inspired materials of the season like pine, berries and pinecones. To make an ordinarily basic holiday wreath more interesting, I use a mixture of pine with sturdy olive and laurel branches to enhance the texture. Pussy willows used in this Hollycroft project provide an unexpected soft gray contrasting color to all the greenery and add wintery interest.

TOOLS

Grapevine wreath base (14" [36 cm])

Wire cutters

High-temperature hot-glue gun and glue sticks (all materials are attached using hot glue unless otherwise specified)

TRIMMED MATERIALS

7 pine sprays (11" [28 cm])

12 cedar sprays (11" [28 cm])

6 olive branches (8" [20 cm])

6 laurel branches (8" [20 cm])

12 red berry branches (6" [15 cm])

12 pussy willow branches (6–12" [15–30 cm])

START WITH THE BASE

1. Attach the pine sprays to the grapevine wreath base using the Spiller Technique (page 23), 3 inches (8 cm) apart.

2. Attach the cedar sprays to the center of the grapevine wreath base using the Filler Technique (page 24).

MAKE IT INTERESTING WITH ACCENTS

3. Bend the olive branches in a gentle "C" shape. The branches should be evenly spaced in the wreath so that the tops are about 7 inches (18 cm) apart. Setting all the olive branches into place before attaching them with glue can help get the spacing just right. Attach them to the wreath with the tops pointing out of the greenery and following the flow of the greenery. When all the olive branches are secured, give the tips another little bend so they aren't sticking straight up at you.

4.   Attach the laurel branches between the olive branches.

5.   Attach the red berry branches evenly throughout the wreath, using a zig-zag pattern so the red berry branches are on both the inside and outside of the wreath.

FINISH THE WREATH

6.   Use the pussy willow branches to add the final finishing touch to the Hollycroft wreath. Attach the pussy willow branches to the outside edge of the wreath, evenly spacing them around the entire wreath, about 6 inches (15 cm) apart.

To hang your new wreath, see page 17 for ideas.

Biscay

SEASON: Winter

SKILL LEVEL: Beginner

FINISHED SIZE: Up to 25" (64 cm) with greenery

The Nordic style originates from the countries of Norway, Sweden, Finland, Denmark and Iceland. This style is minimalist, rustic and natural—perfect for a winter wreath! This Biscay project is special in that it is the only project in this book to use a painted grapevine base wreath. The grapevine wreath painted white lends the design a snowy feel so it can be displayed all winter long. For this design, I also used a special artificial tamarack pine for its short clusters of pine needles to fit into the minimal feel of the design. The wreath is finished with a cluster of large pinecones. For easy attachment, look for pinecone picks, which already have a wire stem attached and are ready for your project.

TOOLS

Grapevine wreath base (18" [46 cm])

White spray paint (use a chalk paint variety for a softer finish)

Wire cutters

High-temperature hot-glue gun and glue sticks (all materials are attached using hot glue unless otherwise specified)

TRIMMED MATERIALS

12 light blue tamarack pine branches (11" [28 cm])

2 dark green tamarack pine branches with pinecones (11" [28 cm])

3 large pinecone picks (4" [10 cm])

START WITH THE BASE

1. Begin this design by spray painting the grapevine wreath base white according to the manufacturer's instructions. I like to do this outside in the yard on a piece of scrap cardboard so you don't need to worry about any overspray of the paint. Begin with laying the wreath down on the cardboard and spray painting the entire wreath. Be sure to paint the inside and outside edges of the wreath too. Let this dry, flip it over and repeat on the other side until the entire grapevine wreath base is painted.

2. When the grapevine wreath base is completely painted and dried, attach the light blue tamarack pine branches. Choose a center focal point on the bottom-right side of the wreath, and attach the branches flowing upward and downward from that focal point, six going upward and six going downward, making sure to overlap the branches so the focal point is covered in pine. Slightly bend the light blue tamarack pine branches in an "S" pattern to give the wreath some shape.

FILL THE WREATH

3. Attach the dark green tamarack pine branches with pinecones in the same manner as the light blue tamarack pine branches, one upward and one downward, bending slightly for a more natural shape.

FINISH THE WREATH

4. Add the large pinecone picks as the finishing touch to the Biscay wreath. Form a Focal Trio (page 26) in the center of the pine with the large pinecone picks.

To hang your new wreath, see page 17 for ideas.

five

From the Field

The field is the perfect blend of wide-open space and sky. There's plenty of room to breathe and feel free. The flowers, bushes, grasses and fruits in the field are in their element. They are perfectly imperfect. They are a bit more wild, rough and all over the place. I think we all kind of long to be unconfined like that, which is why the field is so beautiful.

This chapter puts all that freedom into wreath form. These designs are lush and bursting with texture in all seasons, from the spring greenery used in the Ashby project (page 109), to all the summer wildflowers found in the Hillside wreath (page 115), to my favorite season in the field: fall. The fall field is full of vibrant color and texture from the fruit and pods of the hard-working plants and trees, as seen with the abundance of pumpkins and squash in The Bramley (page 137) and twiggy berry branches in The Cottesworth (page 121). Be inspired by the field to step out and create something unconfined.

the Ashby

SKILL LEVEL: Beginner

FINISHED SIZE: Up to 26" (66 cm) with greenery

Nothing beats a classic greenery wreath. It can be used for all seasons and be placed anywhere in the home to add a bit of freshness. You can even tuck in different flowers for the season or if your décor changes. Even though most of this wreath is green, this design uses a variety of greenery for interesting texture. I like to include a little touch of white Queen Anne's lace in the design to provide some soft contrast to all the greenery. And of course, I include some trailing greenery so the wreath is a little freer.

TOOLS

Grapevine wreath base (18" [46 cm])

Wire cutters

High-temperature hot-glue gun and glue sticks (all materials are attached using hot glue unless otherwise specified)

TRIMMED MATERIALS

8 hanging leafy greenery branches (12" [30 cm])

20 frosted mini eucalyptus stems (7" [18 cm])

7 olive branches (7" [18 cm])

7 white Queen Anne's lace (7" [18 cm])

7 long and 7 short clematis branches (13" [33 cm] and 7" [18 cm])

START WITH THE BASE

1. Begin the base of this wreath by attaching the hanging leafy greenery branches to the outside of the grapevine wreath base using the Spiller Technique (page 23), about 5 inches (13 cm) apart but flowing together.

2. Set aside twelve frosted mini eucalyptus stems for step 6. Fill the center of the grapevine wreath base with eight of the frosted mini eucalyptus stems using the Filler Technique (page 24), lightly layered but covered, setting aside the remaining twelve stems for step 6.

MAKE IT INTERESTING WITH ACCENTS

3. Bend the olive branches in a gentle "C" shape. The olive branches should be evenly spaced around the wreath so that the tops are about 7 inches (18 cm) apart. Setting all the olive branches into place before attaching them with glue can help in getting the spacing just right. Attach the olive branches to the wreath with the tops pointing out of the greenery and following the flow of the greenery. Once all the olive branches are secured, give the tips another little bend so they aren't sticking straight up at you.

4. Trim the Queen Anne's lace, leaving a set of leaves on the stem. Attach the Queen Anne's lace between the olive branches.

FINISH THE WREATH

5. Start with the seven long clematis branches and attach them to the wreath on the outside edge, parallel with the olive branches. Then attach the seven short clematis branches to the inside of the wreath next to the Queen Anne's lace.

6. Fill in any gaps along the outside edge of the wreath with the remaining frosted mini eucalyptus stems.

7. Fluff and bend the hanging leafy greenery to complete the circular shape and create a nice "greenery halo" around the wreath.

8. Take a look at the olive branches and Queen Anne's lace. If the inner circle of the wreath seems crowded and these elements aren't quite centered, give them a gentle bend outward.

To hang your new wreath, see page 17 for ideas.

The Hillside

SEASON: Summer

SKILL LEVEL: Advanced

FINISHED SIZE: Up to 25" (64 cm) with greenery

Ever wanted to just run through a field of wildflowers? To just be carefree, blowing in the breeze and soaking up the sun like the flowers do? This wild-child essence is captured and brought into your home in this Hillside wreath. The key to making this wreath look beautifully wild but not a complete mess is to have a tidy, patterned, evenly spaced design. Stepping back and looking at your progress often helps you to ensure evenness of color and spot any gaps that may need filling.

TOOLS

Grapevine wreath base (14" [36 cm])

Wire cutters

High-temperature hot-glue gun and glue sticks (all materials are attached using hot glue unless otherwise specified)

6 pieces of 22-gauge floral wire (8" [20 cm])

TRIMMED MATERIAL

1 wisteria garland (6' [2 m])

10 pink wildflower stems with leaves (9" [23 cm])

6 large yellow Queen Anne's lace (10" [25 cm])

3 purple flower sprays (11" [28 cm])

8 blue thistles (10" [25 cm])

6 leafy greenery stems (10" [25 cm])

20 lavender stems (10" [25 cm])

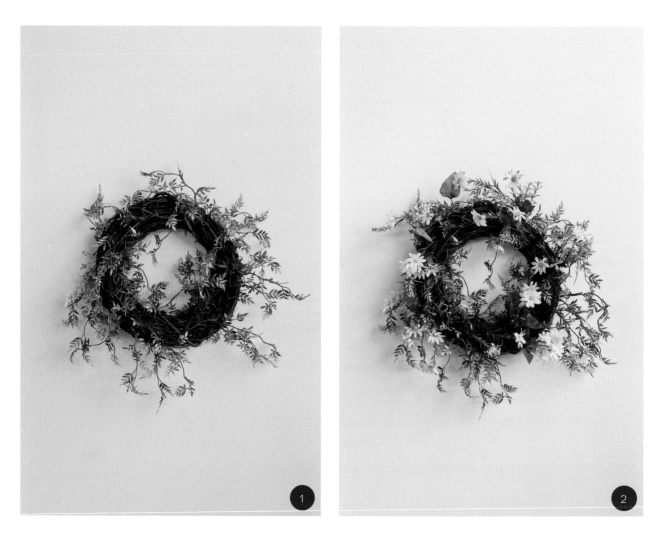

START WITH THE BASE

1. Begin the base by laying the wisteria garland all around the top of the grapevine wreath base. Trim it to size, and attach it with a piece of 22-gauge floral wire about every 6 inches (15 cm) around the grapevine wreath base. Save the extra wisteria garland for step 7.

2. Attach the pink wildflower stems with leaves evenly spaced about 5 inches (13 cm) apart, zig-zagging within the wisteria garland.

ADD THE FLORALS

3. Create the focal point of the wreath with the large yellow Queen Anne's lace. These stems will be attached to the upper right-hand side of the wreath. Begin by placing a large Queen Anne's lace bloom right on the front side on the focal point. Next, add another one below it, and then continue to add the remaining four large yellow Queen Anne's lace blossoms up the wreath and along the side, so the blooms are facing upward rather than facing toward you.

4. Complete the focal flowers by adding the purple flower sprays. Attach one above the first large yellow Queen Anne's lace you attached, one to the right side of that same bloom and the final one going down from the bottom large yellow Queen Anne's lace.

MAKE IT INTERESTING WITH ACCENTS

5. Attach all the blue thistles evenly spaced around the outside edge of the wreath and between the pink wildflower stems with leaves, about 9 inches (23 cm) apart.

6. Attach all six leafy greenery stems around the outside of the wreath evenly spaced as well, between the blue thistles but not blocking the pink wildflower stems with leaves.

FINISH THE WREATH

7. Cut the remaining wisteria garland into 6-inch (15-cm) pieces. Use them to fill in the front of the wreath, just enough to cover any large bare spaces, but feel free to leave some of the grapevine wreath base showing through.

8. Finish your Hillside wreath by adding the lavender stems all around the wreath, evenly spaced out and on both the front and outside edge of the wreath, about 4 inches (10 cm) apart.

To hang your new wreath, see page 17 for ideas.

The Cottesworth

SEASON: Fall

SKILL LEVEL: Beginner

FINISHED SIZE: Up to 35" (64 cm) with branches

The fields worked hard in the summer and now are changing their colors,
rounding out their working season and transitioning to winter. What's left are the
remnants of the season: the last of the berries and pods full of seeds to plant in the earth
for the next growing season. These wonderfully textured elements are stunning in a wreath.
Use all artificial materials for the best longevity. Give all the leaves and stems a
good bend to follow the counterclockwise flow of the wreath.

TOOLS

Grapevine wreath base (14" [36 cm])

Wire cutters

High-temperature hot-glue gun and glue sticks (all materials are attached
using hot glue unless otherwise specified)

TRIMMED MATERIALS

6 fall wheat stems (12" [30 cm])

9 mustard grass stems (11" [28 cm])

9 fall orange eucalyptus stems (10" [25 cm])

7 dried brown pod stems (8" [20 cm])

6 long and 6 short twiggy berry branches (25" [64 cm] and 15" [38 cm])

7 fuzzy wheat stems (11" [28 cm])

START WITH THE BASE

1. Attach the fall wheat stems to the grapevine wreath base using the Spiller Technique (page 23), about 8 inches (20 cm) apart.

2. Attach the mustard grass stems to the grapevine wreath base using a loose Filler Technique (page 24), leaving space for the fall orange eucalyptus stems.

MAKE IT INTERESTING WITH ACCENTS

3. Attach the fall orange eucalyptus stems using the Filler Technique (page 24), alternating with the mustard grass stems.

4. Attach the dried brown pod stems to the wreath, nestling them inside the already-attached filler, and zig-zagging around the wreath, attaching them about 4 inches (10 cm) apart.

5. Attach the long and short twiggy berry branches to the outer edge of the wreath. I like to use the longest, wildest branches on the top, bottom and sides of the wreath, following the counterclockwise spin of the greenery. Then, fill in the empty spaces outside the wreath with the remaining short twiggy berry branches, taking care to bend them into a more natural shape.

FINISH THE WREATH

6. Complete The Cottesworth by adding the fuzzy wheat stems evenly around the wreath to fill in any gaps.

To hang your new wreath, see page 17 for ideas.

The Havenridge

SEASON: Fall

SKILL LEVEL: Intermediate

FINISHED SIZE: Up to 27" (69 cm) with greenery

The Havenridge makes me think of all that overgrown, dead foliage in front
of the creepy abandoned houses you see in scary movie scenes. We take that vibe
and turn it into a sophisticated take on Halloween décor. This design uses artificial grasses,
pods and flowers that look twiggy, gnarled and dried to bring that spooky vibe
without being overtly Halloween.

TOOLS

Grapevine wreath base (14" [36 cm])

Wire cutters

High-temperature hot-glue gun and glue sticks (all materials are attached
using hot glue unless otherwise specified)

TRIMMED MATERIALS

10 wispy tan grasses (15" [38 cm])

21 prickly green grasses (9" [23 cm])

3 skimmia heads (4" [10-cm] blossoms)

3 dried-look sunflowers (3" [8-cm] blossoms)

4 skimmia accent branches (8" [20 cm] long)

6 purple pod stems (11" [28 cm])

3 large and 3 small curly artificial twigs (21" [53 cm] and 9" [23 cm])

START WITH THE BASE

1. Attach the wispy tan grasses using the Spiller Technique (page 23) all around the grapevine wreath base, about 4 inches (10 cm) apart with the grass flowing together as much as possible.

2. Use the Filler Technique (page 24) to attach fourteen of the prickly green grasses to the center of the grapevine wreath base, setting aside the remaining seven grasses for step 8. Some of the grapevine wreath base will show through the prickly green grass.

ADD THE FLORALS

3. Using the Focal Trio Technique (page 26), attach the three skimmia heads to the bottom-right corner of the wreath. This Focal Trio can be more spaced out rather than a tight cluster.

4. Attach the dried-look sunflowers tucked among the skimmia heads, one above, one in the middle and one below the skimmia heads.

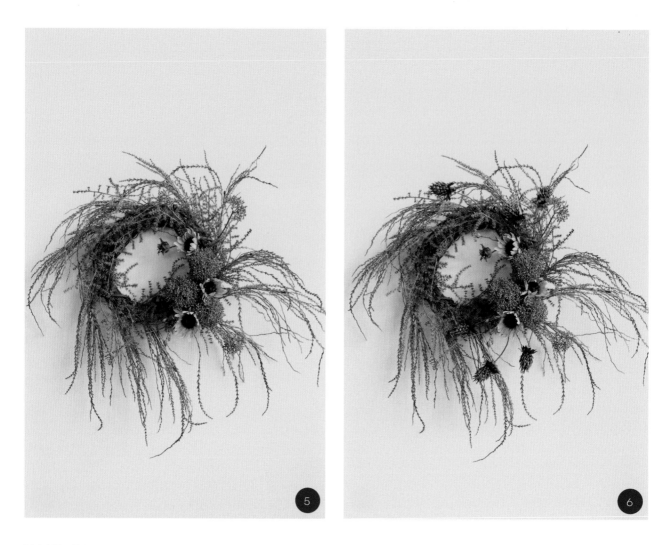

MAKE IT INTERESTING WITH ACCENTS

5. Attach the skimmia accent branches, two at the top and two at the bottom of the focal florals, flowing away from the focal florals.

6. Use the same technique to attach the purple pod stems, three at the top and three at the bottom, between the skimmia accent branches.

7. Give the wreath some shape by using the curly artificial twigs. Begin with the large curly artificial twigs and attach one directly above the focal florals at the top, one at the bottom-right side and one on the bottom. Evenly space the small curly artificial twigs around the outside edge of the wreath to your liking.

8. Use the remaining seven pieces of prickly green grass around the outside edge of the wreath to fill in the design and complete your Havenridge wreath.

To hang your new wreath, see page 17 for ideas.

Gloucester

SEASON: Fall

SKILL LEVEL: Intermediate

FINISHED SIZE: Up to 19" (48 cm) across and 36" (91 cm) long with greenery

Fruit and magnolia leaves are a fall combination for Colonial Williamsburg Thanksgiving décor. Colonial Williamsburg in Virginia is a historical American Revolutionary War period town restored to look as it did back then. I went one year with my family for Thanksgiving and fell in love with the abundance of wreaths and garlands they decorate with all over the town. I wanted to capture that historical mix of materials and give it a whimsical shape found in today's floral design. Past meets present in the Gloucester design.

TOOLS

Grapevine wreath base (14" [36 cm])

Wire cutters

High-temperature hot-glue gun and glue sticks (all materials are attached using hot glue unless otherwise specified)

TRIMMED MATERIALS

12 magnolia leaf branches (about 3 leaves on each individual stem; 9" [23 cm])

3 fall orange hop branches (8" [20 cm])

2 apple branches (a few small apples on the branches; 24" [61 cm])

7 mini blueberry branches (12" [30 cm])

START WITH THE BASE

1. The focal point of the wreath will be the bottom-right corner of the grapevine wreath base. Form a center point in that spot with four magnolia leaf branches, tucking them into one another to form the focal point.

2. Under the magnolia leaf branches focal point, use the eight remaining magnolia leaf branches to add another layer by tucking them tightly under the attached ones, on top, bottom and each side, fanning them around the center.

MAKE IT INTERESTING WITH ACCENTS

3. Attach the three fall orange hop branches in the center of the magnolia leaf branches, tucking them into one another to form a solid focal point.

FINISH THE WREATH

4. Give the wreath some tall shape by attaching one apple branch directly above the focal point and one directly below. Bend the apple branches slightly to give a more natural shape.

5. Finish The Gloucester by adding the mini blueberry branches for a little more whimsy. Attach three mini blueberry branches spread out at the top, one on the right side and three spread out at the bottom.

To hang your new wreath, see page 17 for ideas.

The Bramley

SEASON: Fall

SKILL LEVEL: Intermediate

FINISHED SIZE: Up to 29" (74 cm) with greenery

I look forward to visiting the pumpkin patch every fall and covering my front porch steps in this autumnal fruit. Pumpkins and squash are the telltale sign that fall is here and with it all its glorious festivities. I grow squash in my suburban backyard, and displaying the fruit I've grown is such a joy. This wreath captures the joy of an abundant crop after a summer of dedicated care and shows off the wide variety of this magnificent harvest fruit.

TOOLS

Oval grapevine wreath base (18" [46 cm])

Wire cutters

High-temperature hot-glue gun and glue sticks (all materials are attached using hot glue unless otherwise specified)

15 pieces of 22-gauge floral wire (if needed; 7" [18 cm])

TRIMMED MATERIALS

13 feathery fall orange grasses (14" [36 cm])

4 feathery fall leaf branches (14" [36 cm])

10 large and 5 small pumpkins and squash (4–5.5" [10–14 cm] and 2.5" [6 cm])

14 green eucalyptus branches (12" [30 cm])

8 fall birch leaf branches (11" [28 cm])

START WITH THE BASE

1. Orient the oval grapevine wreath base vertically. The focal point of the wreath will be the bottom center. Create the focal point on the grapevine wreath base by attaching four feathery fall orange grasses, two on either side of the center point flowing down and outward. Attach the remaining nine feathery fall orange grasses evenly spaced going up the wreath, stopping about 8 inches (18 cm) from the top to leave the top section of the grapevine wreath base exposed.

2. Attach the feathery fall leaf branches to the grapevine wreath base, one on both the left and right sides of the focal point and the remaining feathery fall leaf branches evenly spaced up the sides of the grapevine wreath base.

MAKE IT INTERESTING WITH ACCENTS

3. If the large and small pumpkins and squash do not have a pick for attaching, use the floral wire pieces cut to 7 inches (18 cm) to create stems. Use a drop of hot glue on the bottom of each large and small pumpkin and squash and insert one floral wire piece, leaving about 4 inches (10 cm) of floral wire for attaching.

4. Arrange all the large and small pumpkins and squash around the bottom of the wreath to form an abundant bunch. Intermix the small sizes with the large ones and spread out the different colors. The large and small pumpkins and squash should be attached with hot glue nestled together so no large gaps are showing in the bunch.

FINISH THE WREATH

5. Use the green eucalyptus branches to begin filling in the sides surrounding the large and small pumpkin and squash bunch. Attach the branches evenly spaced around the rest of the wreath, flowing outward and downward.

6. Finish The Bramley by using the fall birch leaf branches to fill in any gaps in the greenery around the large and small pumpkins and squash grouping. Evenly space out the branches where needed and attach.

To hang your new wreath, see page 17 for ideas.

Acknowledgments

Many thanks to the following people who helped me tremendously in making this book:

My husband, David, for his unending support of all my entrepreneurial adventures.

Sharon Hughes, my amazing photographer, for making this book come to life with her stunning photos.

Katie Cenkus of Sweetbay Flower Farm in Chagrin Falls, Ohio, for opening her family farm to us for amazing outdoor photos.

Tom and Karen Lunder, my parents, for opening their beautiful home and property to us for lifestyle photos.

Rebecca Fofonoff and the team at Page Street Publishing for believing in me and making this book, my dream, possible.

About the Author

Stephanie Petrak is the founder and owner of Lorraine's Cottage, where she sells her handcrafted faux-floral wreaths and arrangements. Her work has been featured in many Etsy Editor's Picks guides, and she was a juried vendor at the Renegade Craft Fair in New York City, New York; Magnolia's Spring at the Silos in Waco, Texas; and the Country Living Fair in Columbus, Ohio. Stephanie graduated summa cum laude from Lake Erie College in Painesville, Ohio, with a bachelor's degree in legal studies with a minor in entrepreneurship. She and her husband, David, live in the suburbs of Cleveland, Ohio.

Index

A

Adelaide, 41–45

advanced projects, 26

    Adelaide, 41–45

    Eccleston, 47–51

    Hillside, 115–119

    Kinley, 81–83

    Penley, 85–89

AFloral, 16

anemones: Piper, 35–39

apple branches: Gloucester, 133–135

Aria, 67–71

Ashby, 109–113

Avondale, 61–65

B

beginner projects, 26

    Aria, 67–71

    Ashby, 109–113

    Avondale, 61–65

    Biscay, 103–105

    Blomfield, 73–76

    Cottesworth, 121–124

    Florio, 53–58

    Hollycroft, 99–101

    Piper, 35–39

    Wedgemere, 31–33

berries

    Aria, 67–71

    Cottesworth, 121–124

    Gloucester, 133–135

    Hollycroft, 99–101

birch

    Bramley, 137–141

    Sulina, 95–97

Biscay, 103–105

Blomfield, 73–76

blue thistles: Hillside, 115–119

boxwood

    Adelaide, 41–45

    Avondale, 61–65

Bramley, 137–141

bushes, trimming, 21

button leaf: Eccleston, 47–51

C

carnations: Florio, 53–58

Cecily, 91–93

cedar: Hollycroft, 99–101

cherry blossoms: Cecily, 91–93

clematis: Ashby, 109–113

Cottesworth, 121–124

D

dahlias
  Aria, 67–71
  Avondale, 61–65
  Eccleston, 47–51
  Florio, 53–58
  Penley, 85–89
design techniques, 22–26
  Filler Technique, 24–25
  Focal Trio Technique, 26
  Spiller Technique, 23
dogwood: Cecily, 91–93

E

Eccleston, 47–51
eucalyptus
  Aria, 67–71
  Ashby, 109–113
  Blomfield, 73–76
  Bramley, 137–141
  Cottesworth, 121–124
  Eccleston, 47–51

F

faux florals
  selecting, 16–17
  trimming, 21–22
ferns
  Aria, 67–71
  Avondale, 61–65
  Eccleston, 47–51
  Florio, 53–58
  Kinley, 81–83
  Penley, 85–89
fields, 107
Filler Technique, 24–25
floral wire, 17
Florio, 53–58
Focal Trio Technique, 26

G

gardens, 29
garlands, trimming, 22
Gloucester, 133–135
glue gun, 17
glue sticks, 17
grapevine base, 14, 15
grasses
  Aria, 67–71
  Bramley, 137–141
  Cottesworth, 121–124
  Havenridge, 127–131
  Sulina, 95–97

H

hanging techniques, 17

Havenridge, 127–131

heather

    Adelaide, 41–45

    Piper, 35–39

herbs: Wedgemere, 31–33

Hillside, 115–119

Hobby Lobby, 16

Hollycroft, 99–101

hot-glue gun, 17

hydrangeas

    Eccleston, 47–51

    Penley, 85–89

I

intermediate projects, 26

    Bramley, 137–141

    Cecily, 91–93

    Gloucester, 133–135

    Havenridge, 127–131

    Sulina, 95–97

K

Kinley, 81–83

L

lamb's ear: Adelaide, 41–45

large size wreath, 15

laurel: Hollycroft, 99–101

lavender: Hillside, 115–119

M

magnolias

    Aria, 67–71

    Gloucester, 133–135

materials

    selecting, 14–17

    trimming, 21–22

Michael's, 16

N

Nordic style, 103

O

oak: Sulina, 95–97

olive branches

    Ashby, 109–113

    Hollycroft, 99–101

orange hop: Gloucester, 133–135

P

Penley, 85–89

peonies

    Eccleston, 47–51

    Florio, 53–58

pine

    Biscay, 103

    Hollycroft, 99–101

Piper, 35–39

project skill levels, 26

pumpkins: Bramley, 137–141

pussy willow: Hollycroft, 99–101

Q

Queen Anne's lace

    Ashby, 109–113

    Hillside, 115–119

R

roses

    Adelaide, 41–45

    Aria, 67–71

    Eccleston, 47–51

    Florio, 53–58

    Penley, 85–89

S

sedum: Penley, 85–89

silver dollars: Sulina, 95–97

skimmia: Havenridge, 127–131

Spiller Technique, 23

squash: Bramley, 137–141

standard size wreath, 14

stems, trimming, 21

Sulina, 95–97

sunflowers

    Blomfield, 73–76

    Havenridge, 127–131

supplies, 14–17

T

techniques

    design, 22–26

    Filler Technique, 24–25

    Focal Trio Technique, 26

    hanging, 17

    Spiller Technique, 23

    trimming, 21–22

tools, 17

trimming

    garlands, 22

    to size, 21

    by type of material, 21–22

22-gauge floral wire, 17

V

Viburnum: Avondale, 61–65

W

Wedgemere, 31–33

wheat stems: Cottesworth, 121–124

wildflowers

    Adelaide, 41–45

    Hillside, 115–119

wire cutters, 17

wisteria: Hillside, 115–119

woods, 79

wreath base, 14–15

wreath design

    techniques, 22–26

    trimming, 21–22

wreaths, hanging, 17

wreath size, 14–15